Dorothy Davis Collins

Copyright © 2013 by: Dorothy Davis Collins

ISBN-13: 978-0615812199
ISBN-10: 0615812198

Love, Hate & Betrayal

In Loving Memory of

My Beautiful Mother and My Handsome Father

Elizabeth Jacqueline & Theodore Davis

Dedication

I dedicate this book to my immediate family, Annette and James Rivers, Cynthia and Billy Campbell, Frederick and Laura Davis, Kenneth and Judith Davis, a host of relatives and friends who have shown us much love and support during our time of bereavement. Thank you for being there for me and my children, Rubin III, Brian and Kayamia Collins during the up and down struggles which had a significant effect on our lives. I thank all of you with all the love I have in my heart. I also honor my beloved sister and brother, who have gone on to be with the Lord, Gertrude Davis Smith and Theodore Davis, Jr.

By the grace and mercy of God, we are still here and the best is yet to come!

Foreword

As I read the chapter, "When Loving Him Is Not Enough", my heart ached for the writer, yet my soul applauded the courage and intense transparency penned upon the pages of this poignant writing.

I encourage the reader to release your inhibitions and opinions and hear the silent cry of the writer. I believe "When Loving Him Is Not Enough" is therapeutic, as well as life changing and heart healing.

The writer gives the reader an eye opening account of Christianity and character. We're invited in a scene of morality versus His majestic will for our lives. The impact of the lack of intimacy within any relationship is addressed with dignity and how Christ shall love each of us unconditionally.

Dr. BJ Relefourd

Pastor-Vision of Life Ministries

Founder/Visionary- Women of Power

Radio Host-Walking In Power Radio

Foreword

You're a phenomenal woman. There have been many struggles, trials and tribulations, but you persevered, continue to do so. You have set a good example of what it means to do "all things through Christ" and "this too shall pass!"

I have learned so much from you, your desire to tell your story to help hurting women has been your goal for quite a while. Through much prayer and waiting on God's timing, you are there! Dreams do come true!

I have watched you grow, literally as a sister, wife, mother, child of God, friend and now a WOP (Woman of Power). May you continue to grow in Christ and your light continues to shine. I love you Baby Girl!

Minister Annette Davis Rivers

Preface

1 Corinthians 10: 13 "There hath no temptation taken you but such as is common to man: but God is faithful, who will not suffer you to be tempted above that ye are able; but will with the temptation also make a way to escape, that ye may be able to bear it."

I am finding out that whatever I face in life, that God has adjusted me to a perfect fit to the trials and temptations I have or will go through. I have had to realize that just because I am a good person, I am still not immune to the test and trials of this life.

In writing my story, it has brought up a lot of feelings about my childhood, my children, my marriage and the death of my husband of twenty-one years.

Reliving the past has helped me acknowledge the obstacles in my life and how I became victorious over them; regaining my spirit and confidence that was deeply embedded in my soul over the years. It has allowed me to rethink past failures and to finally work through the abuse, abandonment, betrayal and trauma which have been suppressed in my spirit for so long. When the Lord saved me in 1983 he knew my future and what was ahead; for He is the beginning and the end. I now know what he was saving me from. I did not realize my life would be a journey of obstacle courses after my husband died; that I was in a fight for my life. I am forever grateful to the Lord for equipping me with everything that I needed to endure my battles as a good soldier. It was evident in my life that at the end of the battles I realized that I was chosen by God and that my faith in Him kept me in the midst of the fire.

1 Peter 4: 12-14

V. 12 "Beloved, think it not strange concerning the fiery trial which is to try you, as though some strange thing happened to you: V. 13 "But rejoice,

inasmuch as you are partakers of Christ's sufferings; that, when his glory shall be revealed, you may be glad also with exceeding joy. V. 14 "If you be reproached for the name of Christ, happy are you; for the spirit of glory and of God rests on you; on their part he is evil spoken of, but on your part he is glorified."

Introduction

I am reminded of the scripture *1 Corinthians 2: 1 "And I, brethren, when I came to you, came not with excellency of speech or of wisdom, declaring unto you the testimony of God."* I do not consider myself to be profound with words of excellency. If the truth be told, I did not even acquire a college education. I wanted to be a flight attendant, but I could not afford to go to flight school. However, I thank and praise God for the path he has brought me. I thank him for choosing me; a sinner saved by His grace. I count it an honor and a privilege to be used by God. To live by example, through all of my trials, tribulations hurt and pain from childhood to my present age, still standing for the name sake of Jesus Christ. In spite of what others may say or do to me, I am still here. My only desire is to share with anyone who has decided to read this book what the Lord has done in my life, which in fact is my only qualification to write this book. I want to be able to stand before God in that great day and hear Him say to me, "Well done my good and faithful servant". I do not want what Jesus went through for me, dying on the cross, to be a life lived in vain. I want him to be well pleased with me.

I am truly inspired by the words of the Lord which has helped me immensely in my walk with Him. I will admit that it has not been easy; in fact, I will tell you that I have had a rather rocky life thus far. I use to think that I was an accident because I was not in the plan of my parents Theodore and Elizabeth Jacqueline. There was a five year age difference between my brother Kenny and I. My parents thought they were finished having children, however, I was baby number seven. I did not realize why my life entailed all that it had until the Lord saved me at the young age of twenty-one, the prime of my life; now I am of legal age to do as I please from the world's point of view.

I was blessed by the Lord before and after he saved me. Meaning He would not let me end my life as a teenager when I could not erase the many thoughts of being molested sexually as a child and how I longed for my mother's love after she died when I was seven years of age. I felt I was missing a very important part of my life; the leading and guidance of my mother's wit to help me as a teenager, to face the challenges which were confronting me. However, I do believe she prayed for me as she was dying that the Lord would keep me and watch over me. When my mother died at such a young age of 33 of breast cancer, I felt alone and abandoned while longing for her love. I look back over my life from my childhood until now and I know that I have been blessed.

Before my mother's passing, there was a day that I will always remember. The day that I stole some money that was to pay for our health and life insurance. It was just like yesterday, "Dot, Dot, I hear her calling, I reply, "Yes Mama", I knew that I was in trouble by the sound of her voice. She said, "Come here right now! Yes mama, I said in fear. She knew I had taken the money and there was no need for me to wonder if she knew I did it. As I looked up in her face feeling so ashamed and scared at the same time, she asked the dreaded question. "Dot, did you take the money out of the envelope for the insurance man? No mama, I positioned my mouth to lie, such a big lie, because I did not want the wrath of mama to lay a switch to me. Back in the day you had to go get your own switch, it was like a death walk. You knew not to come back with a small one. The crepe myrtle trees we had in our yard was the choice pick for mama. It is amazing how mothers know when a child is not being honest, but I guess it was a dead giveaway when I came home from the country store with a bag of cookies and candy. She knew I did not have any money and that I had already asked her for money earlier when I saw her putting the money in the envelope and she told me that was all she had. I said to myself she would not miss it. How stupid and naïve I was: I was only seven and I thought I would not get caught. Well, to this day, I can still remember that spanking. As I can remember, my mother was a beautiful, gentle, and stern lady and I have missed her terribly. I felt she was too young to die at the age of thirty-three, and I felt that I was robbed of my mother bonding with me. Although I was only seven, I can remember certain things about her. I can remember her telling me to always do what was right and tell the truth. Do not lie or steal were the two words that were programmed in my mind. Down through the years those words still remain. I thank God for giving me a godly mother who I only knew for a short period of time in my life. I will always cherish what she and my father instilled in me, moral values.

I thank God for helping me to remember what she told me when I was too young to really understand. I would always fear that I would not live to see 33 or even the age 43 which I am now, to see the beauty of my children, to watch and see them grow up to aspire and achieve to be great men and a great woman of God. There is no greater joy other than the new birth of your soul and spirit, but to see the joy that your children bring into your lives. I am ever so grateful to the Lord for my children and my heritage; I would not be who I am today without God's grace and mercy.

I thank God for my father who passed away April of 1995. He was a strong black man; tall in stature that I looked up to. He was a great provider. A man who made sure that even if he had to work two or more jobs we would never go without. We always had what we needed, not so much what we wanted. He taught me so much about independence; to take care of yourself with the help of the good Lord. He was not a man of many words, unless of course he had a few drinks in his system. I will always remember him saying, "I pay the cost to be the boss", however, he did not phrase it quite so nice. I can remember the time when my life was almost ended at the age of twenty. It was a night which I will never forget. There were only two people who were aware of my pregnancy, my sister and her friend. Someone told my dad before I had the chance to. I remember Rubin and I sitting on the couch watching television when my dad beckoned me to come here. The next thing I knew he had a gun in my face. To this day I do not like guns and have never had a desire to own one. My life literally passed before my eyes, I thought that man was going to kill me that night. Rubin did not know what to do, whether to run or stay, but he stayed. That was quite an eventful night. I am so thankful that the Lord saved my dad before his passing.

As a wife and a mother of three, I strived to be the godly woman that God had chosen me to be; to be the wife, companion, soul mate and friend to my husband.

Aspiring to be the mother that my children would rise up and call me blessed. I longed to be a great mother to my children for I was unfortunate as a child to have lost my mother at the age of seven, so I cherish the moments I have had with my children. You often wonder if your best was ever good enough, asking yourself the questions, "Did I tell them the right things?" "Did I set a good example for them?" "Did I love them too much or not enough?" As a Christian mother, I believe I did all of the above well, but as it is with our daily walk with Christ, we are ever learning to do and to say all the right things. I was blessed to have my children at the young age of 21, 22 and 23.

As a working mother, it was not easy raising three children born one year behind the other. It was quite a challenge for my husband and I. You want to always be there for your children to train them up in the fear of the Lord, to guide them in the right direction, but sometimes being there is not enough.

When children reach their teenage years, sometimes they become rebellious, trying to usurp your authority. It seems as though it is harder to reach them to give them sound godly advice. You awaken one morning and you look at them and you listen to them talk and you ask yourself the question, "Who's children are these?" The things that they say, the things you would not think that they would do, especially coming from a Christian home, but their actions let me know that our enemy, the devil, is out to destroy the unity of the family.

I have learned and I am still learning that you must stand on the word of God no matter what the circumstances are, knowing with all assurance that the victory belongs to Jesus Christ in every situation which comes before us as children of God.

Ephesians 6: 11 – 13, v. 14... and after you've done all to stand, stand therefore…. We must stand against our enemy no matter what. Sometimes it seems as though he has gotten the upper hand, but I know in the end that the truth always wins.

My husband and I tried to instill in our children to do what is right and pleasing unto the Lord. To fear the Lord and no matter how bad things may get, that if you trust and obey the Lord, he will bring whatever the problems may be to pass.

Sometimes I feel as though I failed being a mother, especially when the children disobeyed their father, me and most importantly the Lord. We have instilled biblical teachings in their lives since they were babies, but as soon as they became of age to rebel, they did.

The devil was waiting for his opportunity to bring chaos in our lives, and boy did he bring it! From drugs, pre-marital sex, teenage pregnancy and self-centered attitudes; thinking of what we can always do for them.

I was so naïve in thinking that our children would not betray my trust because I was always there for them and lived godly before them, but the devil does not care who you are. I thank God that he has spared their lives and I thank him for the strength to endure until they were on their own. I will never give up on my children. I will always pray for them to become godly men and a godly woman for Christ. I look back on my life and see where he has brought me from and feel assured that he will do the same for them.

I will always cherish the book by Dr. James Dobson, "Parenting Is Not For Cowards". Oftentimes it is a spiritual warfare between children and their parents, but as parents, we can never give up on our children, we must continue to pray and look for guidance and comfort in the Lord.

There were times when I did not know quite what to do, where to go or who I could talk to. But, there was the Spirit of God deep down inside of me which has always kept me aware of my surroundings and guided me in the right direction even before I was saved. Not that I did everything right, but when I did wrong, I had a conscious to know I did wrong and to ask the Lord for forgiveness.

On my journey with the Lord, I am learning each and every day that all I have encountered or will have to come face to face with, I can rest with all assurance that the Lord already knows about them beforehand and he has made a way of an escape for me.

If there is anything that I can expound on, it is that there will be battles great and small in this walk with the Lord, but He has equipped us with everything we need to do battle with the enemy, satan. With Jesus Christ as my guide and counselor, it is my prayer that this book may be a blessing to someone other than myself.

Table of Contents

The Move

I had no idea that the move to Clermont, Florida would bring about drastic changes in our lives when we believed that we needed a change, a fresh start from Eaton Park, Florida. We did not realize that this move sent us directly into the enemy camp. Personally, I believed the move would help our marriage. Rubin was struggling to remain in the church, alcohol was winning the war, and when it came to being considerate of me and the children, it seemed as though his blood family, mother and siblings won every time. The children were teenagers and we knew that they could adjust to making new friends. Unfortunately, they made friends with the wrong type of environment. Although they were being raised in a Christian home it seemed like they did not learn anything we tried to instill in them or absorb any of what was being taught in church. They adapted to the wrong environment way too fast and that is when the trouble began. You can say hell was breaking loose and so many things were beginning to go wrong in our home with our youngest son Brian and our daughter Kayamia. The oldest, Rubin, was the only one at that time who seemed to hold on to the teaching the longest, (so it seemed) Things soon changed with him as well during his senior year in high school. My rose colored glasses were shattered, our home was falling apart.

Prior to my husband and I agreeing for me to stay at home, we made an investment. It would have paid us enough money to follow our dreams: for me to be home when the children came in from school. I so admire families who are able to have one parent to stay in the home with the children as they are growing up. I believe it makes such a difference in their lives. My desire was to become a wedding and events planner while involving him and the children in the business. However, I had some doubts. I thought it was too much to get into debt over if it did not work out. Since he wanted to do this, I agreed to go along with his decision. We were in this together.

When you hear the expression it sounds too good to be true, it usually is. Take heed. Little did we know that this was another attack from the enemy. He used the people of God in a big way. So many people lost so much. The investment went south like a bungee jumper without his or her rope not secured correctly. Reality set in that I was without a job since I had already resigned from GMAC after twenty years. We dropped from a family income of about $60,000.00 a year to about $30,000.00, with three children, a new home and now a second mortgage since we took a loan for the investment which fell through. It was very difficult to find a job that paid me the salary I was getting at my Corporate 500 job, but we seemed to be making it alright with the job I later obtained. But before I could get a steady job, the finances were shot; I was juggling one paycheck to keep things afloat. Our credit went from "A-1 to very bad". For several months the finances were not good.

In my juggling act, I used the money Rubin's sister paid us for the rent on the home we still owned in Eaton Park. In trying to pay our bills, things got out of control. We were just struggling to keep up. More chaos reared its ugly head, two payments were lost in the mail and now a third one was due on the home in Eaton Park, and two payments on the home in Clermont. I thought to myself, no problem, the income tax check is due to arrive any day. Once it did, we would be able to catch up on everything; at least I thought we would. The next thing I hear is a knock at the door; it was the sheriff department serving us papers for non-payment from the mortgage company. On top of that, they also served papers at the home in Eaton Park to Rubin's sister. How do I know? She called me. She was highly enraged. As I tried to explain to her that everything was going to be taken care of, she was so upset and would not calm down, so I had to just hang up on her. Oh what a mess this led to. I thought I was going to lose my mind.   I felt as though my head would split wide open, then I thought it would be okay if I died and had a heart attack and go home to be with the Lord.   This is when I first found out the loyalty my husband had for me, which was none! He sided with his family against me. They tried to have me put in jail for forging Rubin's signature on his checking account, when in fact he was the one who gave me the check book to pay the bills. He did not want to handle the responsibility of paying them with only one paycheck coming in. The juggling act was very unnerving. I was furious. I had to call his pastor to make him and his family discontinue with what they were trying to do to me and our family. Oh the drama! Time passed but the tension was now there in our marriage and the togetherness had somewhat dissipated.

In the meantime, how do I stay focused when all hell is breaking loose in my home? Crying out to the Lord day and night, praying that things would level off. Just when you think everything is going to be alright, satan gets even busier. My husband has turned against me, I am not finding employment quick enough and he is blaming me that we are about to lose everything.

At this point I'm about to give up the ghost.

Psalms 55: 12 – 14 "For it was not an enemy that reproached me; then I could have borne it: neither was it he that hated me that did magnify himself against me; then I would

have hid myself from him: But it was thou, a man mine equal, my guide, and mine acquaintance. We took sweet counsel together, and walked unto the house of God in company."

With my husband and my in-laws conspiring against me, I did not expect him to hang around much longer. For I do not believe he had ever learned how to handle pressure unless it was from a bottle of alcohol.

My daddy always instilled strength and perseverance to all of his children, to never give up. I believe that my husband was a victim of too much love from his mother; he had never been able to turn loose her apron springs. I had no problem with him loving his mother, I admired that about him.   She had more clout with him than I would ever have. Forget leave and cleave. I had never been able to get much from my husband, not even as much as a compliment. He never told me if I looked good or if I was beautiful to him. He never commented on what I wore; I always tried to look my best for my husband. I believe that you are an extension of your mate. He was just the opposite; he did not really care what he wore or what he looked like. He had never been able to console me when I was hurting. He never even asked me what was wrong if I was crying. Seldom or never did he even try to communicate with me on issues which confronted our marriage. He never wanted to talk about the hurt from his past. Oftentimes, I wonder if the child Rubin and Jennifer gave up when they were young had an effect on him. I can only imagine the pain of having to go through life not knowing your first born or even where they are in this world. I could not understand why they gave the child up when they eventually got married. I believed the marriage did not last because of differences they encountered as an interracial couple. At times I felt that the reason he was not loving towards me was because of the things he endured with his first wife. I felt as if I was paying for the past, the baggage. For him not being able to have closure on his past I believe really hurt our marriage for years. There were so many secrets about my husband I feel that I will never know, and maybe it is for the best. There were secrets that we should have shared, but his mother was the one he chose to share them with. We had just got home from

Georgia the night I can recall being awakened from my sleep from the sheriff department knocking at our door at 3 a.m. and them arresting him for lewd and lascivious acts. They took him with no shirt and no shoes.

Thankfully, the children were asleep, but were awaken by the voices of the police officers. I had them to stay in their rooms. He said it was not true, but I never got the full story from him. I wanted to go to court with him, but he did not want me to, however, he let his mother accompany him. What did that tell me? It was none of my business. I was dreadfully hurt and my heart ached. I just knew he did not want me to know the full truth, thinking that I would leave him if the allegations were true. Obviously they were true because I found out later that he ended up paying fines to a probation officer, I discovered the cancelled checks for payment. And if I am correct, you do not pay fines for anything if you are innocent.

I often wondered why I stayed feeling like a fool. It was not like I did not fulfill my wifely duties. That was never a problem, we were young and sexual. The question is why is it that men or women feel the need to cheat when the other spouse is being faithful? What went missing?   Marriage is a joy and a privilege that God has ordained. Why can't we be real with one another and hide nothing with the devil?

I have always been the type of person who has tried to be a help to people and not so much as to please myself. I have sacrificed a lot for my family by always trying to be there for them, to make sure that they had what they needed and yet I felt that I was not appreciated. Somewhere down the line I lost the person I once was by trying to be whatever everyone else wanted me to be. But I know in doing my best for others that God is pleased with me. Even though it hurts so badly when no one ever bothers to think of my feelings, I am grateful that the Lord has placed inside of me the strength I need to be able to absorb the pain, which only He could do. And no, I am not super woman, I just believe in the supernatural power of God.

I think back to the words of wisdom from my late pastor Apostle Henry Ross Sr. when I would seek counsel about our marriage especially in the early stages. He would always tell me "Sis. Collins, you have to learn how to adjust". I would say to him I was not the one in the wrong, why should I have to adjust? He is the head of the family. He would then proceed to tell me that I was stronger than I thought. I begged to differ.

I would have never imagined that my husband who I dearly loved would hate me to the extent of talking against me with his mother and her agreeing with him calling me names and him not defending me. His mother was very special to me. I made sure she received her Birthday, Mothers' Day and Christmas gifts every year. I treated her like the mother I never knew wishing my mother was still alive. I could not believe I heard what I heard when I picked up the receiver of the telephone to say hello to her one night. I could hear her bashing me telling Rubin he better not get another job, saying that I need to get off my fat butt and get a job.

I had struggled with my weight for some time, and that comment was like a knife in my spirit. Never have I been hurt in such a hateful way. I felt as though a part of me had died. I thought I knew her and I thought she loved me, but obviously I was so wrong. I sit here and wonder why I took such abuse. All I know is that I want to stay saved and do what is right, and right now I have no choice. No job, no money, but I know within my spirit that this too shall pass.

The Power of One's Tongue

James 1: 26 "If any man among you seem to be religious, and bridleth not his tongue, but deceiveth his own heart, this man's religion is vain."

James 3: 5 – 8 V. 5 "Even so the tongue is a little member, and boasted great things. Behold, how great a matter a little fire kindleth! V. 6 And the tongue is a fire, a world of iniquity: so is the tongue among our members, that it defileth the whole body, and setteth on fire the course of nature; and it is set on fire of hell. V. 7 For every kind of beasts, and of birds, and of serpents, and of things in the sea, is tamed, and hath been tamed of mankind: V. 8 But the tongue can no man tame; it is an unruly evil, full of deadly poison."

When I was accused of having an affair with a deacon at the old church where I received the gift of the Holy Spirit. I was devastated. I was so naïve in believing that people, your brothers and sisters in Christ, could be so cruel. This indeed was a testing of my faith.

When my husband came home one night from church, vividly, I can remember sitting on the side of the bed and he spoke these words, "I heard you're messing around with Deacon so and so". He looked at me with anger and contempt. As I looked at him and could see the rage in him, I said, "Who told you that lie?" He wouldn't tell me, and I then found myself getting angry as well. I wanted to know who my accusers were. I believed it to be very cowardly of them not to come to me if they saw such a thing. I began thinking to myself, surely he does not believe this lie, but his countenance showed me that he did. I was so upset and hurt. I told him, "You can believe what you want to believe." I did not try to defend myself because I knew the truth and so did he if he wanted to be honest about it. He saw me every day, day in and day out. I went to work, church, and back home. When did I have time to have an affair, especially to be seen in Georgia at a truck stop of all places?

How could he be married to me for so many years and still not know who I was and the type of person that I am. I had only showed him my undying love no matter what. This was another blow to our already rocky marriage and again he was not there for me.

The rumors spread like a wildfire. Every time I went to visit my old church in Lakeland, it no longer felt like my home. The looks, the stares, I just did not feel loved or cared about. Instead, I felt like a woman with a big "S" on her chest, although I hadn't committed any sin. My character was shattered. But I held on to my integrity and refused to let my heart be filled with evil retaliation. I could not understand why this had come upon me, but I knew I had to take it all in with a grain of salt and do the best that I could do before the Lord.

1 Peter 4 12-13

V. 12 "Beloved, think it not strange concerning the fiery trial which is to try you, as though some strange thing happened unto you: V. 13 But rejoice, inasmuch, as ye are partakers of Christ's sufferings; that, when his glory shall be revealed, ye may be glad also with exceeding joy."

I thought everyone knew me as the faithful sister, altar worker, pastor's assistant, usher, choir member, friend, the devoted wife and mother. I thought they knew that I would and did do anything I could for others and the church I so loved.   I was so outdone. I could only ask the Lord, "Why me?" And He said to me, "Why not you?" Again, I had to reach deep down inside and pull out more faith and more of Jesus love.

I was truly being tested at this point. Out of all the people I considered to be my church family, there was only two people who confronted me on the matter, Dee Dee and Diane. I am thankful for their confidence in me as their sister in the Lord.   There were others who came to visit me, but I can vaguely remember if all were genuine or just being nosey. That was the way I was feeling about my church family while grieving for my husband.

(Galatians 6: 1 "Brethren, if a man be overtaken in a fault, ye which are spiritual, restore such an one in the spirit of meekness; considering thyself, lest thou also be tempted.")

All the others continued to spread the gossip even way up in Ohio to my best friend that I grew up with, Doris. Oh, how sad!

Mark 11: 26 "But if ye do not forgive, neither will your Father which is in heaven forgive your trespasses."

I truly had to pray and forgive the person(s) who sent forth this terrible lie, a lie that I feel was the defining factor in our marriage which I believe led my husband not to care about his health to get better. I believe he said to himself, what is the point. I believe he just gave up on life. The one thing that could make him feel that way was to believe that his wife no longer loved him, which was the farthest thing from the truth. Oh how my soul ached. I had to forgive in order for me to move on with my life.

Proverbs 11: 21 "Be sure of this; the wicked will not go unpunished, but those who are righteous will go free". I believe that when the wrath of God does befall the individual(s) who told this terrible lie, I will not gloat or rejoice, but I will know that I have been avenged.

Romans 12: 19 Dearly beloved, avenge not yourselves, but rather give place unto wrath: for it is written, Vengeance is mine; I will repay, saith the Lord. Proverbs 19: 5 "A false witness shall not be unpunished, and he that speaketh lies shall not escape."
No matter what punishment I feel that the individual(s) deserve, it is out of my hands and in the hands of the Lord. This battle is not mine to fight, but it is the Lord's.

Ephesians 4: 32 "And be ye kind one to another, tenderhearted, forgiving one another, even as God for Christ's sake hath forgiven you."

There have been times in my life where I have gone through so many trials and tribulations but the Lord has always brought me out. Lately my trials and tribulations have surmounted heavily around me.

You hear people say sometimes that they are going through so much and they ask the Lord the question, "How much more Lord?"

We have to believe on the word of God which says in ***1 Corinthians 10: 13 "There hath no temptation taken you but such as is common to man: but God is faithful, who will not suffer you to be tempted above that ye are able; but with the temptation also make a way to escape, that ye may be able to bear it."*** and even at the hardest or the lowest times, we have to count it all joy.

James 1: 2- 4 "My brethren, count it all joy when we fall into divers temptations; Knowing this, that the trying of your faith worketh patience. But let patience have her perfect work, that ye may be perfect and entire, wanting nothing."

We must trust and believe in God. *Hebrews 10: 35 "Cast not away therefore your confidence, which has great recompence of reward"* and in doing so we can cast down doubt and fear and release faith and hope.

For it is impossible to please the Lord without faith as stated in *Hebrews 11: 6.* Sometimes it is hard to see what the end of a certain situation will be and that is where we have to focus in on our faith in the Lord; for the just live by faith. We must not lean to our own understanding but acknowledge the Lord in all things no matter how big or how small the matter may be.

Proverbs 3: 5 & 6 "Trust in the Lord with all thine heart; and lean not unto thine own understanding. In all thy ways acknowledge him, and he shall direct thy paths."

When the dark clouds are hanging over you for a long period of time, you feel as though you have been cursed. You do not feel the presence of the Lord anywhere, as though he has turned his back on you. We must encourage ourselves and know that when our burdens are the heaviest to bear and we feel that we are walking alone, it is then that the Lord is carrying us.

I could not write about these things unless I could testify to them myself. You can go through life hearing many testimonies about the goodness of God; how he has brought different people out of difficult situations. You can hear many encouraging words, but until you have gone through difficult times yourself, you will never know or experience the awesome power of God. It is not enough to know of God, you have to know who God is in your life.

How Did I Make It Over? My Soul Looks Back And Wonder!

1Corinthians 10: 13 "There hath no temptation taken you but such as is common to man: but God is faithful, who will not suffer you to be tempted above that ye are able; but will with the temptation also make a way to escape, that ye may be able to bear it."

I'm finding out that whatever I face in life, that God has adjusted me to a perfect fit to the trials and temptations I have or will go through. I have had to realize that just because I am a good person, I am still not immune to the test and trials of this life. When I look back over the years of my life, I can only wonder, how did I make it over?

My mother dying when I was only seven years old, feeling abandoned by her and my father when he shipped me off to live with my oldest sister to help raise me. Being sexual molested at the age of ten, moving back home to live with my father at the age of fourteen. I started at a young age cooking, cleaning, laundry and yard work. It was just me and my dad; my brother had gone off to college. I tried to kill myself as a teenager because I felt so alone, abused and misused. Going through life feeling like damaged goods.

I can recall my father being unbearable at times when he was intoxicated. He was mostly a man of few words when the alcohol was not talking. In some ways I do not think he ever got over my mothers' death.

I can remember not dating until I was out of high school. I think mostly because my self-esteem was shot when it came to boys. I thought they were out to take advantage of me and I could only reflect back to being molested. I also felt I was not attractive compared to the other girls in school. After high school there were a couple of losers in my life until Rubin came along. He was nicer than the other three guys I knew for a short time. Rubin and I were as different as night and day and I did not think that we were right for each other, but I could not get rid of him.

He said that he loved me the first time he met me, but I don't know if he really knew what love was. I became pregnant, and I still tried to get out of the relationship, but he would not give up on it. He was the only one of the three guys I dated that my father actually liked. He was the only one that could get my father to talk when he was sober. I felt pressure from Rubin to marry him because I was carrying his child. I did not want to for just that reason, however, I gave in. I knew the morning after I said "I Do" that I did not come before his mother. He left me in the bed at our hotel to go help his mother clean her offices. Here I was six months pregnant and alone. I could only wonder, "What have I done?" After Rubin III was born, a couple of months later I was pregnant again with Brian and the following year with Kayamia. Three babies in three years, what was I thinking? I can only thank the Lord for saving me before Brian was born. He saved me from my insanity. I know it was the grace of God that kept me from being overwhelmed. Here I was a fulltime working mother, homemaker, wife, and involved in the ministry by the age of twenty-three. We were always traveling with the "church"; it was our life. There was hardly any room for anything else until the children were older and begin getting involved in school activities; football, basketball, cheerleading, track, piano lessons, children's choir. Somehow I did not feel overwhelmed. I know it had to be God as I reflect back. I am thankful that my husband was there to share in the load. I know if he had his way we would have had more children. During the delivery of our first child I had complications. I can recall overhearing my pediatrician tell my ob-gyn doctor if she had waited to see if I could have the baby naturally, that she would have killed us both. You would think after that scare we would say that is it, no more children. We proceeded to have two more the next two years. Yes, you read it right; three children in three years. Whew! After three cesareans I decided no more cutting on my body in spite the way he felt about it and the way he perceived the church's teaching; be fruitful and multiply. I'm so grateful to the Lord for keeping me and giving me the strength to endure in growing up real fast.

Hebrews 11: 6 "But without faith it is impossible to please him: for he that cometh to God must believe that he is, and that he is a rewarder of them that diligently seek him.

Ephesians 6: 16 "Above all, taking the shield of faith, wherewith ye shall be able to quench all the fiery darts of the wicked.

Being strong and having the mind to go on is a matter of choice. When turmoil presented itself, I knew I could not run towards the door looking for the easy way out, I knew I had to hold on to my faith in God and hang in there for the long haul. The promises of God are not on auto pilot, they must be pursued.

I knew I had to be diligent in seeking God using my faith in him against the mountains in my life. Many are the afflictions of the righteous, but the Lord will deliver them out of them all.

There have been many Pharaohs in my life who have tried to hold me back. But I know I cannot stay where I am, I have to continue to dig deeper and go further in the Lord. I have had to learn how to shake off certain things and people and get into true worship and praise God. I know that I have to keep praising God until something happens, until I receive a breakthrough. I will not turn loose until he blesses me. I have had to realize that my righteousness could not stop the pain, hurt, or the accusations which came upon me. I knew I had to hold on to my faith to make it through. When you have been hurt by your church family, it can be quite devastating, and in my life it was. It was so unexpected and it caught me off guard. I had to let this experience mature me and push me into my destiny by the grace of God. It has made me what and who I am today, a much stronger daughter in the Lord.

The experience allowed me to see that there is life after every obstacle that I was confronted with. I had to move on from yesterday and rejoice where I am today. I cannot let yesterday hinder me for what is in store for me today. I have had to let God know that I am ready to walk into my destiny in spite of what people have said about me, or have done to me. I know that my best is yet to come. I had to die to self; that I did not retaliate, that I did not become bitter, for out of the heart flows the issues of life. As Jesus has said in the word, *Matthew 10: 28, "And fear not them which kill the body, but are not able to kill the soul:"* My prayer is that the experiences that I have gone through will be a blessing to someone else to learn from; to let someone else know that you can make it too. I have learned by praising God, that he will move things for me.

I cannot let anything or anyone try to hinder me from getting to my destiny, I have to shake it off. When I get tired and feel like I cannot go on I have to keep stepping out on faith. However, you cannot make it with faith alone, you have to pray. Nothing can be substituted for prayer.

You must have a prayer life. It will break every yoke. It does not just change things, it changes everything. When we stop taking the time to fast and to pray, seeking the Lord at every given chance that we have, that is when satan starts to work on us double time. He knows when we get weak along the way. He knows just when to strike.

He will continue to eat at us on the issues of life which he knows will throw us off balance. But we have to remain in that secret place as it is written in ***Psalms 91:"He that dwelleth in the secret place of the Most High shall abide under the shadow of the Almighty."***

I do not want to be just a survivor in Jesus Christ; I want to be a success in Him. I know that I can face anything and anyone as long as Jesus is on my side. For I also know that no one cares or loves me as much as Jesus does.

When I look up at my mountains in my life, I have to keep looking up to the Lord and know that my help comes from Him who made the heavens and the earth. ***Psalms 121:1-2 "I will lift up mine eyes unto the hills, from whence cometh my help. V. 2 My help cometh from the Lord, which made heaven and earth.***

It is God who will keep me and not allow me to stumble or to fall; it is my God who watches over me at all times. I will bless the Lord Oh My Soul and His Praise will always be in my mouth no matter how long the devil continues to buffet me by trying to throw me off course.

My faith is in God. My trust is in God. I may not have much materially, but I have what matters the most, peace of mind. No matter how much money you may have, it still cannot buy you peace of mind.

Oh Daughter of Mine

Our first two children are boys and since they both were cesarean births, we prayed that our last child would be a girl. And thanks to prayer, she was a girl! A lot of people would often ask my husband and I where did we get the name Kayamia.

I can recall one night we were reading the bible when I was pregnant with Kayamia in the chapters of genealogy. Her name just appeared, although we knew it was not in the bible. That is when we knew in faith that we were having a girl. She is our gift from God as well as our sons Rubin and Brian.

As she blossomed, she became more beautiful on the inside as well as the outside. She has a pure heart; always trying to help others when they are in need, or just needed a friend to talk to. Who would have ever thought that this beautiful child, being the apple of our eyes would have a worm eating its way to the core? All of the kids were great children until we moved them from a sheltered environment to an environment which became detrimental to their lives as well as ours. (You always want to protect your daughters more because the majority of the time the boys could pretty much handle themselves.)

Kayamia became quite a challenge to her father and I when we moved to Clermont. She rebelled early because she did not want to move. She got involved with the first young man she came in contact with and went against us telling her that she could not be involved with him. She deliberately defied our authority and so did this young man.

You think you have done the very best when it comes to raising your children, having their best interest at heart. And in doing so, we believed we pleased the Lord, serving him to the best of our ability. However, satan is always seeking whomever he can devour. He attacked us at our most vulnerable moments. The move was a change we all had to adjust to, but I believed it to be the hardest for Kay.

I love all my children equally and would do anything I could for them as long as it was in line with the word of God. It was my mission to be the mother to my daughter that my mother was unable to be for me. I made sure that we did the mother and daughter things. We had our girls' day out where we went out of town and stayed at the hotel; we went swimming, shopped and dined out. It was just a special bonding time for us.

They say an idle mind is the devil's workshop, so I tried to keep Kayamia active in the church choir, cheerleading, piano lessons, track, modeling and television. She did modeling and television after the move to Clermont; she was doing well in it, going on auditions, being an extra for Universal Studios until she rebelled with this young man.

She got to the point that she would not listen or do what her father and I said. I tell you the truth, there was days when you knew why some mothers of the wild ate their young. Things began to happen; she was sneaking out of the house, stealing the truck to go see this young man we had forbid her to see, trying to commit suicide, sneaking him in the house.

When I knew that she was being sexually active I took her to the doctor to be placed on birth control. I knew as a Christian mother that she was to remain abstinent, but I also knew she was not being a Christian at the time and we had to do something. We were already struggling financially whereas we did not need any more burdens with teenage pregnancy. But who would have ever thought that when I took her to the doctors that she would refuse to be put on birth control. It did not matter that she was a minor living in our home that we could not make her go on them because of the law; she had rights. I was thrown for a loop! Later, I found notes where she had written to the young man telling him I was tripping for trying to run her life and trying to put her on birth control! Oh how she rebelled! Of course it was not long after that that she became pregnant at the age of fifteen.

Moreover, then came the drama with the young man denying that the baby was his. This went on and on until the baby was born and she came into this world looking like her daddy's twin. She was the spitting image of him.

There were times when something was going wrong with the children and the Lord would always wake me in the middle of night by ringing the door bell. And wouldn't you know that was when the trouble was happening, when everyone was supposed to be asleep. That is just like satan to wait until the right time to attack when our guards are down, coming in like a thief in the night.

There was the time when she allowed this young man in our home and the Lord woke me to go check the house. I could hear noises in the bathroom, hers and the young man. That is when the dead bolt lock had to be changed out on the pool door to the bathroom. Another time was when I received a phone call from the sheriff department asking me if I knew that my truck was in another town, I knew that Rubin our oldest son had come home from work in it and he was in bed. However, Kayamia was missing in action. Her bed was empty. So I asked the deputy the address where the truck was parked and wouldn't you know it was at the young man mother's house. So off we went to go pick up our truck and our daughter. Of course, there was a scene; Kayamia did not want to come out of the house for she knew the rod was not being spared that night. His mother wanted to blame us, and my husband and I wanted to blame her, but in the end we knew who was to blame, satan. He was just sitting back watching and laughing. When we finally got her home, I gave her the whooping of her life, but it did not really make her do any better. She rebelled even more. It was not like we spanked our children all the time; only when it was a serious issue. As her mother I was really hurting in my heart to know that the child I bore could turn out this way. I wanted so much better for my daughter!

That's why I always tried to be there for her as well as her brothers. I missed that with my mom. Even trying to keep her involved in church and outside activities, she still would not or could not see that we love her. The biblical teaching and living examples did not matter at this point in her life. I just never imagined in a lifetime that my daughter would ever be this way. The young man she was determined to see was always in and out of trouble with the law. What is it about some girls wanting these bad boys? There were times where my husband and I would try to witness to him about the Lord, but it seemed to go in one ear and out the other.

When we said she could not have phone calls or visits from him, she would spitefully use the phone or he would continue to keep calling the house all time of the day and night.

I knew he was trouble but it seemed like even prayer could not make him go away. On top of all the drama with Kayamia, her dad was diagnosed with diabetes. So now we are dealing with her rebellion and Rubin's illness. The boys were pretty much behaving. Thank God for that!

After Kaylianna was born, the drama continued. Her birth was a happy one and a sad one. I did not want my daughter in the situation that she was in. Having a baby at sixteen, unwed and making me a grandmother at thirty-nine (smile). But mostly having a child from someone who was not good for her well being.

Days after we brought Kaylianna home from the hospital, I was once again awaken by the Lord earlier than usual for work. I go to check on Kayamia and the baby and the young man is there trying to force himself on her, she was scared and crying. I want you to know, I did not let the Holy Spirit stop me from going ballistic on this young man. I succeeded in kicking him out of the house myself.

It always seemed like I was the only one dealing with the drama when Rubin became ill with diabetes. It was like Rubin wasn't concerned about living anymore. He was not working and was spending more time with his mother and siblings. We were married, but I felt so alone! The drama continued with Kay and the young man. We went from the house phone ringing off the hook to taking out restraining orders on him. It was just madness with a capital "M". He was not taking care of the baby financially or any other way. The burden was falling upon Kayamia, her dad and I which we could not afford, but had no choice in the matter.

Kay worked throughout her pregnancy while the lazy boy did nothing to support her. He was still going off and on that Kaylianna was not his, just looking for any excuse not to give support to their child. She came into this world looking just like him, there was no denying it. (If he had a problem with thinking that Kaylianna was not his, he should not have put his name on the birth certificate. Why wait until after the fact when now she has your name?) There was on again - off again restraining orders, which went with the on and off again relationship with the two of them. She finally confessed to me that she was afraid of him and that is why she did not enforce the restraining orders. It took about a year and a half after Kaylianna's birth, before Kayamia decided to move on. This proved much harder than we hoped. The young man became very possessive, jealous and angry. Finally, on one particular night, it cost him his freedom. He ended up in jail, but he was only in there for four months this time. Sadly, it did not change him, he continued to harass.

Journal Entries

There were on and off times when I would make journal entries and as I look back on these entries, it was painstaking to re-read. In reading these entries one can see the battles which I was confronted with. I felt as though I was on a never-ending rollercoaster ride. To fight or not to fight for the survival of my marriage. However, I pray that it may be helpful to someone else who may be going through similar situations.

February 18, 2002

Father, I need you this very hour. I don't know what to do but to remain focused on you. As I sit here at the dealership waiting to see how much it is going to cost to get the van fixed one more time. I am so tired of having to do things for and by myself when I am suppose to have a man in my corner. But these days am more alone than ever. There are even some days when I feel that you are not even with me, but I know that you must be, or I would not be still standing. I now know that if you do not help me no one else will. I am depending on

you Father. I come before your face with
thanksgiving and praise in spite of all I am
going through. I can only wonder Lord what
am I not doing for you that has bought these
hard times on me or is this just something I
must go through? I know I have not been the
servant that I know I should and could be, but I
am trying to stay focused on you until my
change has come. I have been with Rubin for
almost twenty years, we have had many of
hard knocks in our marriage but it has never
been as bad as it is right now. I do not see
where it's going to be or get any better.

  If I am the problem Lord, please help me and
if we don't work things out, help us to remain
non-hostile with one another. It is now
apparent that his mother and the rest of them
are more important than me and ours. I cannot
and will not compete with them. So much has
happened that I do not think it can be repaired.
Who would have ever thought that we would
be in this state? I keep thinking on how much I
have put into this marriage. I have endured the
mental abuse, which I believe is almost worse
than physical abuse. Lack of communication,
trust and intimacy. It has been four months
since Rubin has touched me and even when I
confronted him about it, he wants to shift the

blame on me, saying I was the one who did not want to be touched. Taking his random trips to Lakeland makes me believe he has someone else. Fine if he does, but have the decency to let me know that he wants out of this marriage. I just want him and I to be happy, even if it means not being together. It is time to just move on. I wish he would just be a man about everything and stop being a mama's boy.
These last two years have been two years I am ready to put behind me and move on. I do not want to dwell in the past but look for a brighter and better future. I am looking for greater things in the Lord. If I can just get ahead. Father help! Well it is about eleven p.m. and it is time to go to bed. I pray for strength and a brighter tomorrow.

Father I need a new vehicle, $3000 is a lot of money which I do not have to get this vehicle repaired. I feel so alone and abandoned. I often wonder if anyone else would or could find me attractive. My heart feels sick and Father I need to be healed. I have so many emotions running at the same time, I have so much I need to do and I do not know where to begin. I need another vehicle, medical coverage, a healing for my heart. Father how can I help others when I am so emotionally sick within my body. Father I need wholeness in my spirit where I may please you. Please help me. People say that times are getting worse, but I can only believe that for God's people that it is getting better all the time. It is satan's job to put out illusions in the spirit realm to try and discourage the saints; but I know without you Lord, I am nothing and can do nothing without you. Keep me Father!

Goodnight

February 19, 2002

I awaken at 2:45 a.m. this morning unable to go back to sleep. My mind became fixed on Rubin wondering what I could do to help him. I don't know if the Lord showed me this or is it just my imagination. Could it be that he was molested as a child and he has some pinned up emotions where he cannot trust anyone to release them. I often wonder if that is the reason why he does not care too much about himself, is it the reason he cannot care about me the way I desire him to, is it the reason why he clings to his mother the way he does? I know I cannot compete with her and I am not going to try. I just wish he could trust me enough to let me in to help ease the pain. I have a deep compassion for him and I want the best for him. I have invested twenty years in this relationship and I do not want it to go down the drain. I want to salvage my marriage if I can only if it is the will of the Lord, however, it does takes two. I want His will to be done. I see my husband in so much pain and it hurts me to no end that I am unable to help him because he feels he cannot let me in his heart completely. I wish I knew what was going on with him.

I cannot shake the feeling that something happened to him in his childhood where he will only let you in so far.

I want to help him. I want us to have a blessed life and a blessed marriage. We made some financial mistakes but I wish we could have worked them out as husband and wife. Well Father, it is 11:30 p.m. and it is time for me to give you thanks for another day. To ask you to forgive me of my short comings. Help me to see the joy in the suffering. Lord I ask that you will bless me to fast for my family. To gain strength to stand against satan and all of his wickedness. Bless me to stand in the gap for my family. I love them all with all my heart. Some days I get weary and feel that I cannot go on any further and then you send someone along to bless my soul. Thank you Father for loving me.

Lord bless me to stand in gap for my in-laws who seek to destroy my family. Save them Lord in their wickedness. Bless me Lord to stand for your name sake no matter what comes or who goes. Help me to endure to the end that I may be a blessing to someone in need. Thank you Father for a heart of understanding. Thank you for saving me and thank you for my foundation.

February 20, 2002

Father God, when and what do you know not to pray for? I do not know anymore if I am supposed to pray for a relationship. Lord I am at a standstill; I just do not know what else to do. I feel so alone in my natural state, but I thank you for your holy spirit. Help us both to be free of this bondage which has held us both down, not reaching the fulfillment we could have in this marriage. Fix it Lord. Much Love!

February 21, 2002

Well it is bedtime and I have not written anything today. What a day, but I did have time to sing praises from my heart and knowing that you are still with me. No matter the outcome, as long as you are still there God, nothing else really matters. I know that I have been a good person, good wife, mother and friend. I thank you for a compassionate spirit. Sometimes I think too compassionate. I can cry so easy at the dumbest things and the sweetest heartfelt things. Keep me Lord and may I never neglect to keep you on my mind and in my heart. Lord I feel sometimes that I have failed you cause I am not doing all that I should be doing to the glory and honor of your name. Some days I just do not know what to do. So much confronts me these days where I am too timid to make a move. Strengthen me Lord; guide me in the right direction. Help me to love you more and never to doubt that you will always have my back as long as you are in my life. Bless me as only you can. Bless my family and my in- laws who I feel are against me and look to cause more problems. Bless those who bless me and curse those who curse me. Help me to love myself. I am beginning to have self-doubt in myself. Am I good enough, pretty enough, sexy enough, I just do not know. I know I must diligently seek you and seek first your kingdom and righteousness and then I can have what I need and want in you. Help me Lord. Much Love!

February 24, 2002

Well Lord after the ordeal I had last night, I really do not know how much more I can take! I could not believe Rubin and his mother were on the phone bashing me. From trying to help people and being kicked to the curb it seems to me that it just does not balance out. Lord I need your guidance for I really don't know what to do or say anymore and I can only wonder if not saying anything makes it worse. Lord I am ready to move on and make a new life for myself, forgetting the past. You cannot teach old dogs new tricks if they do not want to learn. Lord I know I must guard my heart for the enemy is out to destroy me by using whoever or whatever he can. But I am determined to make it Lord regardless of the journey. Lord if you see me failing at the wayside, I pray that you just bring me on home to be with you. For nothing and no one is worth me losing my soul over. Relationships don't matter, friends, and family, only you Lord. It seems all of my life I have had to suffer in one way or another and I am so very tired. Nevertheless, I still hope in you Lord.

February 25, 2002

Today I went looking for a used car and did not find anything. Before I could even get back to work, the van stop working on me again. Thank God I was right across the street from work. I thank you Lord for my employers, who have blessed my life. For them to be so gracious, kind and so understanding through all I have been through and going through. I do not know what I would do without you Lord. I can only wonder why my husband is being so cruel and disloyal to his family. To put his mother and siblings before his own.

February 26, 2002

Well Lord, again I come to you in disbelief of how evil people can be. I am now being accused of having an affair with Deacon So and so and that people have seen me with him in Georgia at a truck stop! How cruel can people be? I have been married to this man for almost twenty years and how can he think that I would betray him the way he has betrayed me.

I know the hurt it brings when you have been deceived by your spouse, why in Jesus name would I betray another woman in that way? I can truly say that I have loved this man and tried to do anything I could to please him and our children. I know within my heart that I have only tried to make our house a home. I feel so betrayed and abandoned by him. No trust is left at all. Why should we keep pretending to be happy when we are not? I have been faithful since we have been married. Even through the hard times I have remained faithful regardless of what anybody may think, say or believe. Lord you know my every move and you have account of all my thoughts and actions, you will be my judge and jury. Furthermore, when have I had time to have an affair? Between working and babysitting, going to bed by eleven every night. Him seeing me day in and day out. I spend my weekends with my daughter and granddaughter. Lord have mercy on whoever is trying to curse me through these false persecutions. Keep me Lord, continue to hold me up.

Bless my home and my family. I do not want to feel any animosity towards Rubin, his family and my church. Just bless them Lord to do right by you.

Love you Lord!

February 27, 2002

Thank you Lord for the challenges this day that you have helped me to prevail through. Tomorrow is a big day, a big step. I pray for your guidance that I have made the right decision to end this charade of a being happily married. I just want to be strengthened in you and release the weight of what is in my way. I want to be free of anti-trust, no communication, and no intimacy in this relationship. I pray that you strengthen me to go through what is ahead for me and that I remain focused on you. Bless your people Lord. Deliver us Oh Lord from the error of our ways. Love you much!

February 28, 2002

Well I went to the lawyer today and was advised to do the divorce first and then the bankruptcy. When Mrs. Freeman told me that it only takes twenty days for the paperwork to go through and three minutes for the judge to end a twenty year marriage, I was beside myself. I am forty, married over half of my life and I feel so out done. I keep asking myself did I waste too much of my life trying to save a marriage which has been on shaky ground as long as I can remember; even when he was arrested last June. I am really wondering now if this is the way the Lord would have wanted me to go or did I go through all this pain needlessly. One can only wonder.

As you have read, February 2002 was a very trying month and the rest of the year was not any better, I will not burden you with those details.

Death of A Stranger

April 24, 2003 along with the dates April 23 and April 25 will always be etched into my heart until I leave this earth. Rubin died the morning of April 24, 2003, the day after our twenty-first wedding anniversary and the day before his forty-eighth birthday. I asked the Lord on several occasions how could this have happened?

I can remember the night before his death, Kay had gone to McDonalds to get us something to eat and I went into our bedroom where Rubin was sleeping to see if he wanted the sandwich that Kay had brought back for him. He was cleaning out his wallet and drawers of papers, tearing them up and placing them in the garbage. He said I will eat it later. Then the phone rang and it was his pastor asking if he needed a ride to church, I handed him the phone and I overheard him telling his pastor he was not going tonight. It never dawned on me until later that he had a feeling that he was not going to be here much longer.

I found out from my next door neighbor that Rubin told him that he did not need him to bring the paper over to him when he was finished with it anymore. He had given his car to his pastor for one of his sons. I could not fathom why he would do such a thing when he had children on his own who needed a vehicle. My heart ached knowing he had time to make things right and refused to do so with me. I was furthermore devastated by his actions when it came time to make funeral arrangements and my sister Annette and I go down to the City of Lakeland Risk Management Office to get the information on the life insurance and to find out that I was not the beneficiary. When I was employed with GMAC it was mandatory that the spouse was your beneficiary. However, with the City of Lakeland, I was informed that it was not that way and he could list whomever he pleased as the beneficiary. He had listed his mother. My heart sunk even further and the tears were uncontrollable. Did he hate me and the children that much?

The day my sister Annette and I went to make the funeral arrangements, I told the mortician that I could not afford the cost of the funeral. I told her that we would have a memorial service and have Rubin cremated. I later received a call from the mortician that his mother was going to pay for the funeral. His mother did not know or maybe she did, that I was made aware of the fact from the City of Lakeland that she was the beneficiary.

She continued to lie to our children that I had received the insurance money and they needed to ask me about it. I could not believe the audacity of that woman, his family! Do you really believe that I would have to give up my home and voluntarily surrender my vehicle to the company I used to work for and file for bankruptcy if I had received the insurance money which was due to the children and I? I could not believe it! Oh the anger I had felt towards my husband. How could he leave us this way!!!

When Loving Him Was Not Enough

I felt emptiness in my marriage for a long time before I established an intimate relationship with the Lord. My intimacy with the Lord came about when I laid on my face and cried out to Jesus with all my heart in the first Women's Retreat I attended with my old church, Greater Refuge Church of Our Lord Jesus Christ, under the leadership of the late Apostle Henry Ross. It was at that retreat where I learned how to pray; to go boldly before the throne of my Father God and let my requests, my hurt, and my pain be known before Him.

He already knew my heart, but he wanted me to come to Him with all that my being held. I became complete in Him at that moment in time. I learned that if I would love Rubin as Christ loves me that my love would compensate what I was missing from him. Where I lacked the intimacy I needed and desired from my husband, Jesus stepped in. He filled the void, whereas I learned to cope without true intimacy from my husband.

I desired more than a sexual relationship with my husband, I longed for a love affair; I do not believe he knew what love really was. If he did, he did not portray it towards me.

He never knew how or just did not want to open up and share his true feelings with me. We never really had a deep love affair. Everything seemed so artificial and I can only wonder why we stayed in the relationship for so long. I believed I was a good wife and friend to my husband, and a good mother to my children. I tried to treat my husband as My King, but he would not let his guard down. He was too afraid to show his true emotions to me even if I gave him any compliments; in return I did not feel completely appreciated, wanted or needed by him.

I learned to deal with it for the many years we were together. It has almost been a year and I still miss him so very much. Sure, we had our differences in our marriage, just as everyone does, but it still does not ease the pain of his final departure with no closure. We were having marital problems, which resulted in us sleeping in separate bedrooms, which was my choice to do so.

I lost all respect for him as my husband and the protector of our family the moment he allowed our daughter's estranged boyfriend to come into our home and drag her out of bed and take her outside while screaming for her father to help her. When I think about it, it brings tears to my eyes, because a father is suppose to protect their children, especially their daughters. He did nothing but go back to the kitchen table to read his bible (that is right, his bible). Oh the rage I felt. I had to take it upon myself to go outside with a butcher's knife and promise to kill him if he did not let her go. That night I was like a momma bear protecting her cub.

It was then that our enemy satan began to work on destroying our home for good. I became so tired and frustrated of being hurt, not physically, but mentally and verbally when it came to him choosing sides against me with his mother and siblings. I only realized when it was too late that I had done exactly what satan wanted me to do by removing myself from the bedroom.

Ephesians 4: 26 "Be ye angry, and sin not: let not the sun go down on your wrath: v. 27 "Neither give place to the devil." Well the sun went up and down for nine months because I was not wise enough to see what I was letting the devil do to us. I became weary and tired, because I was blindsided by the lack of protection from Rubin. When he died suddenly we were living separately in different bedrooms. I felt that if I did not give in that things would have gotten better that he would be the one to say enough is enough let us make things right.

However, that was not the case. I dealt with that guilt for quite some time until I came back to the realization that I had to give the guilt over to the Lord, get the help I needed from Him so I would be able to release it.

The last year and a half of our marriage was very rocky. Although at times we were civil to each other as long as I did not say anything about him putting his mother and siblings before the children and me.

Right before Rubin's death there were days
when I would come home from work and he
would not even acknowledge my presence with
a hello or how was your day unless I said
something to him first. The hurt was
indescribable. I felt then that the love had
really left the relationship. Day in and day out
he would sit at the kitchen table reading his
bible; I mean daily; going to church every
Sunday, Monday, Wednesday, and Friday or
whenever the church doors were open. I could
not believe he could not even manage to speak
to me and say, "honey can we talk?" I never
loved someone so much in my life that would
be gone overnight. Sometimes I feel by me
being so acceptable to the way things were,
just coping with it year after year, after year, it
got to the point where I just got tired of it all
and put up a wall as well as he did. We just
shut each other out.

Being left as a widower at the age of forty-one, a marriage of twenty-one years, I feel as though I do not know which direction I am to pursue. A part of me is missing and I know I must go on, but it is just hard. Will I ever be able to love again? I believe I gave most of my heart to one man already, of course with Jesus being the man in my life first spiritually, but the natural man is gone. I tried so hard to please him, making sure the home was clean, the children were fed and clothed properly, being a sexual woman for him when he needed it. How do you go on to love someone else when the one you loved for so many years, half of my life, is gone and you feel like even loving him was not enough? How big is the heart? Is there enough room for another mate? Although it is too soon to even think of such a matter, however, one can only imagine.

No one but the Lord will ever know the hurt and pain I am still feeling and going through, and he has been gone for almost a year now.

Prior to me selling our home, sometimes when I was in the kitchen, I still expected to see him come out of the room and ask me, "babe, whatcha cooking in here?" or if I was in the family room watching television he would ask me what I was watching. Seldom would he sit down and watch with me unless it was sports or if I was watching the animal channel with our granddaughter Kaylianna. He loved his granddaughters, Kaylianna and Aysia. Kaylianna lived with us since we brought her home from the hospital and he was always fascinated when she would do something new or get all up on him or under him. I can still hear him say "whatcha doing gal?" She would just make him smile, which I loved to see especially with his missing tooth on the side.

I think back when he did not want to get the tooth worked on at the dentist, he rather that they just pulled it out even though it could have been saved with a root canal. He was a simple man, no fuss kind of guy. When it came to going to the dentist or even wearing nice clothes, he was most comfortable with his t-shirts and tennis shoes. Even when it came to going to church, I had a problem with that when we first got married, but I learned to get over it and love the man for who he was. He was for the most part in many ways a man with a gentle and caring heart, but also a very stubborn man set in his own ways. He was not one to ever buy me things or the kids unless it was sports related for the boys. He loved sports. When it came to the kids, the house, vacations, him or myself, I purchased the things we needed or sometimes wanted.

He paid for the roof over our heads, which he said, was his **only** priority. He never went out of his way to do nice things for me. I can recall one time when I needed pantyhose for church and I asked him for some money, he would not give me the money, he went in the store with me to pay for them to make sure that was what I was going to get.

I never even received flowers from him and he knew how much I love flowers. It would get under my skin, but I learned to deal with that too. God gave me the grace and wisdom to go through many of the challenges we faced in our marriage. Some people often wondered why I continued to accept so much less in the marriage when they felt that I deserved more. I did not care what other people thought. It was simple, I loved my husband and I took our vows seriously: until death do us part. Trust me, it got so bad sometimes before his death that I told him he could leave if he was not happy. It seemed as though we were both so miserable, partly because he became ill with diabetes; losing sight in one eye, it is like he just gave up on us and life. He was not able to work at the job he had with the City of Lakeland so he was put on permanent disability. I tried to be there for him, by taking him back and forth to the doctors until his mother and siblings took over which came by way of misunderstanding.

It got to the point where I was taking him out of the network area of doctors into another county because his older sister felt compelled to tell the primary physician that he was not taking care of her brother properly; she was going to contact the medical board and the Better Business Bureau. The doctor felt threatened and dropped Rubin as a patient; therefore I had to do more driving time. I was taking off from work to take Rubin to the doctors and I was not getting paid for missed hours. I asked him one day for money for gas and money to put back in my check to replenish what I was losing to pay the bills that I needed to pay for the house. He in turn told his family that I could not keep taking off my job to take him to the doctors. The only reason I asked him for the money was because he was still getting paid from the city where he worked.

Lack of communication played such a major part in our marriage. In our marriage, we never really talked about the serious things. Rubin was not big on talking. He would always shut down whenever I asked him anything about his past or his childhood. I would try to talk to him until I just had to say just forget it. If there were important issues about the house, bills or the kids, if I did not see things his way, I was wrong and my contribution did not seem to matter. At times I did not feel like his wife, more like his slave, his do girl. It was though my opinion did not matter about anything. I tried to look beautiful on the outside as well as stay beautiful on the inside but it just did not seem to matter. I cannot express the importance of being able to talk to one another. Two becoming as one, oh what a big statement. Sometimes hard to do when there is no communication or trust. A feeling of loneliness comes over you like a big black cloud. I believe whole heartily in marriage, which is ordained by God. It is such a beautiful unit when you work together as one. I considered my marriage my ministry; forever trying to please my husband, as unto the Lord.

I am such a compassionate person and I loved to show my vulnerable side to my husband but it was often stagnated because he did not know how to be passionate or romantic, which I believe stems from his childhood. It is my belief that husbands and wives should be in agreement for the marriage to sustain. *Amos 3: 3 "Can two walk together, except they be agreed?"*

In our marriage we have often had disagreements and it was always about money or his mother. And since we were in such financial despair, things began to escalate. As I tried to hold on to my faith that God was going to bring us out in due time, my husband was pulling away from me and against me. In trying to maintain a good attitude about things it seemed as though it was not working. I knew that I could not lose my hope in the Lord. *Psalms 121: 1….* I believed that if the Lord did not work things out for our family, then it could not be worked out.

Surely the devil is not going to help us unless we sell our souls to him and there is no guarantee with a liar, him being the father of lies, the originator of them. ***John 8:44 "Ye are of your father the devil, and the lusts of your father ye will do. He was a murderer from the beginning, and abode not in the truth, because there is no truth in him. When he speaketh a lie, he speaketh of his own, for he is a liar, and the father of it."*** You know he will sell you short. He will never let you see the consequences of your actions until it is too late. So I will carry my cross with the Lord. I longed for some time for my companion to confide in me and I in him, someone to love me unconditionally through the bad times as well as the good. Lord, how I needed a godly man who feared the Lord and who would take charge as the head of the family, not relying on his wife to always handle things. I was so overwhelmed with burdens, trying to juggle money to pay this bill or that bill. I am at the point where I cannot juggle anymore. I keep petitioning God to help me for I feel as though I am going under water for the last time, my legs have become weary from dog paddling and my arms are tired from waving for help. I do not see a ship in sight and my faith is slowly drifting away. It was like I was in a daze. Then

I come back to my senses. I say to myself, how can I possess anything from God if I have the wrong spirit? I know that God will not bless me if I am not in the right attitude, because I would not be portraying Him. So I try to remain focused on the word of God and stand on His promises. ***2 Peter 3: 9 "The Lord is not slack concerning his promise, as some men count slackness; but is long suffering to us-ward, not willing that any should perish, but that we all should come to repentance."*** I have to hold on to the words that He will never leave or forsake me.

The Aftershock

In starting over what is the first step? Lord only knows. It just seems as though I am standing still at this point in my life where there is so much I have to do and be for others that I do not even have the time to start thinking about myself. I have had no time to grieve for my loss.

So much has happened since Rubin's death; (still so hard to believe every time I say it) Kayamia joined the army. Rubin went to jail and my youngest son Brian was having so much trouble with his baby's mama drama. Me having to file bankruptcy, losing my job and taking care of a two year old, just imagine. I could not believe how my husband left things with our family in debt.

Not giving thought to how the children would feel and what they could only imagine how he felt about them, giving the life insurance money over to his mother, and her not even batting an eye to accept it. And giving his car to his pastor knowing his sons could have used it.

As a mother and grandmother, I would never let my children leave their spouse or children without anything. Not caring if they survived financially or not. More hurt, more pain, but mostly anger and bitterness. I did not know that he felt the way he did about me, so much hatred. Moreover, for what reasons? Lord knows all that I ever tried to do was to love him, our children and make our house a home. I never gave him any reason to doubt my love for him. Although he wanted to believe rumors about me from our so-called Christian church family, which were so ridiculous that, I could not even believe that he would have even entertained the thought. Oh what a letdown. There had been things that people said to me about him, but I refused to believe; for one, I never saw it, and two, I loved him. I thank God for His spirit of forgiveness.

I know that I would not be in the right frame of mind today if I hadn't forgiven what was done to me by Rubin. Surely it was not easy. I was not so holy than thou that I did not become angry or bitter, considering the state I was left in.

It was not enough that he left me without making amends in our marriage, he left us with the feelings that he did not really care about us first and foremost. It is still taking time to get over the betrayal, hurt and the sting his death left behind. I can only thank and praise God for keeping me closed in my right mind, helping me to hold on to the hope in Him.

There are some days when I look back on what happened and all I can say is Lord, Thank You! I could not have made it this far without you. It's still hard financially, but the Lord is meeting my needs.

Oftentimes I lay awake in the bed talking to the Lord. I make my plea unto Him, Lord keep me; do not let me fail you. I have to remind myself and the Lord of His word that he has never seen the righteous forsaken or his seed begging for bread.

Psalm 37: 25 "I have been young, and now am old; yet have I not seen the righteous forsaken, nor his seed begging bread."

I cry unto Him saying, "Lord I have been faithful, I have treated people right, I praise and glorify your name, please help me out of this turmoil that I am in financially, spiritually and physically.

I wonder how much longer I will have to suffer with this affliction. I am trying to be the daughter you have called me to be, I am living holy, I praise you, I am faithful in my tithes and

Dorothy Davis Collins

offerings, but yet I still suffer. I can only hold on to the scripture... "Many are the afflictions of the righteous, and the Lord shall deliver him or her out of them all." I know that I must hold on to my faith no matter what. I know that I must stay focused; I know that I had to forgive those who falsely accused me. I have had to be wise enough to let the Lord fight my battles and in doing so; I know that I will come out victoriously.

2 Timothy 3: 12 "Yea, and all that will live godly in Christ Jesus shall suffer persecution."

I am waiting on the Lord to do extraordinary things in my life which in turn He will receive all the glory due to Him from me. I must admit there are some days that it looks pretty dark and dreary, but I know that I must continue to wait and wait patiently on the Lord. There were times when I was so lifeless, I was weak and had no might in me. But I thank God for encouraging me to just hold on, knowing that He was on His way.

Isaiah 40: 29 "He giveth power to the faint; and to them that have no might he increaseth strength."

I must not be anxious for anything, but wait on the right timing of the Lord.

Longsuffering is not my favorite Fruit of the Spirit, however, I thank God for being with me in my time of suffering.

Galatians 6: 9 "And let us not be weary in well doing: for in due season we shall reap, if we faint not."

Runaway Daughter

Kay and I did not know how sick her father was. He kept so much from us. We could not understand how he could live in the same house with us and not tell us how sick he was. She had to be the one to find him lying dead on our bedroom floor.

At the time my husband and I were sleeping in separate bedrooms. I can remember her knocking on my door, me beckoning her to come in, that the door was open. I always left it unlock in case Rubin wanted to talk. The look on her face had me scared. I asked her what was wrong. She said, momma you need to go check on daddy. He is lying on the floor. All of this was happening so fast. I run to the other side of the house, knelt down trying to wake Rubin up, to no avail, we call 911. It seemed like they took forever, but they were there in a matter of minutes. They immediately begin to work on him.

I go to my room to get out of my pajamas so I could be ready to ride in the ambulance to take Rubin to the hospital, but as I was coming down the hall one of the paramedics met me to inform me that my husband did not make it. I fell to my knees with a squeal, NO----------------!! At the time it was just Kayamia, the baby and I at home. The boys were not living at home anymore. I called for the boys to let them know that their dad was gone. They immediately came to see him before he was taken away by the mortician. Kay and I were devastated.

She blamed herself thinking she heard a scream in the middle of the night and did not get out of her bed. She was torturing herself with the thoughts if she only had gotten up to check that she could have saved her dad. I had to let her know that God is in control of everything. If it was meant for him to be alive that God would have kept him that way until help arrived. She had no power whether he lived or died. With him being as sick as he was, that he was in a much better place now.

The guilt and the blame got the best of her. She went off and joined the army without my approval or knowledge of it. She was trying to run away rather than deal with it in the place where she was loved.

She thought by getting away, that it would help better her and Kaylianna's lives and help me financially considering the way her dad left us without anything. I also believed she was running away from all of the baby daddy drama. I would rather she would have stayed home and we deal with the situation which we were faced with. However, off to the army she went four months after her father's death. Neither of us had enough time to grieve. It was too soon for her to be leaving or to leave me with Kaylianna to raise until she came back from Korea. Before she could even leave for Korea, tragedy once again reared its ugly head. He finally snapped. He kidnapped her and sexually assaulted her. He ended up going to jail on Christmas Eve, 2003. He was later sentenced to six years for her attack and on other drug related charges that they had on him.

In dealing with her being thousands of miles away, her grief period had began to sink in. She is calling and crying, continuing to blame herself for her dad's death. For me not being able to hold and console her was difficult. I was trying to get through the grieving process as well, take care of Kaylianna and I was financially overwhelmed.

I was a basket case myself, but I had to keep a smile on my face and one in my voice to try and help her. After a few months she begins dating someone new.

She finds herself searching in the arms of another man trying to find love and compassion instead of relying on God to help her get through the hurt, pain, bitterness and abandonment. I felt in my spirit that he was not the one for her. Once again, she had to find out in a way which was devastating to her.

A month after her return to Korea after being home for Christmas, the man she was in love with was stabbed to death in her room by a fellow soldier. I never would have believed that my daughter would be going through a similar situation that I had gone through, losing a close companion. I never thought that she would be going through so much at such a young age. Oh how I wished that I could have protected her more as her mother. I had someone tell me that I was hurting her more than I was helping her by staying with her father through all the mental abuse, settling for less. If that was the case, I am sorry for the pain this may have caused her even though it was not my intention. I took my marriage vows to heart. I looked at my relationship in all its extremities as an opportunity for God's glory to come through. I believed that if I did all that I could in my marriage to the best of my ability that God would bless my marriage. All I ever wanted was for my daughter as well as my sons to see God through me.

True Friends

When my husband died, I found out who my true friends really were. Jeff and Debbie Schwenneker really had my back. I believe with all my heart that they were truly god-sent. They have always portrayed as having the spirit of servant-hood ever since I have known them. Doing whatever they could for others. They are more than my employers, they are my friends.

I can remember the morning when we found Rubin lying on the floor not knowing at the time that he was dead. While waiting on the ambulance to arrive, I can remember calling Jeff to tell him what was going on and within a matter of minutes he had arrived at the house to see about us. I can recall him telling me that he wasn't leaving us until someone else arrived who loved us as much as he and Debbie did. So he did not leave until Debbie arrived.

Aside from my family, I have never experienced so much love from people who will always be in my life as well as their children who have shown me so much love and kindness. They have helped us in so many ways, spiritually, financially, emotionally but mostly just being great friends. When I lost my job in February of 2004 after Jeff resigned, his old partner did not want to keep me on because I was so close to Jeff and Debbie.

Things began to get pretty bad. I was able to collect unemployment for a little while until my car began to give me trouble and I was not able to get to jobs. So when I told the truth about having car troubles to the unemployment office, the unemployment stopped and they wanted me to pay back some of the money. How was I able to do this without a job or a car?

It became clear that I could not afford to keep our home so I ended up selling it and moving to Fort Myers to live with my sister Annette and her husband James. I stayed there for five months until the opportunity presented itself for me to move back to the Orlando area. Kay was due to come home for Christmas and I wanted to have had a place by then for her to come home to but that was not the case. So the next best thing came along, Jeff's Aunt Penny asked me to come live in her home since it was empty while she was recuperating over at Jeff and Debbie's home. Here I was again being blessed through this family.

After looking for jobs to no avail, it had become apparent to Debbie that she needed help in the office part time. So they asked me to come and work for them. I was hired back working for them in February of 2005, one year after my departure from the old job. It was quite a year. Since they were working from the home and I was living across town with Aunt Penny, Jeff and Debbie invited me and my granddaughter Kaylianna to come and live in their home which we did for about a month until I found a house to rent.

Living with them for that month was a blessing. I believe we became more like family rather than friends. Their love and hospitality towards me will always be cherished and never forgotten. They will always have a special place in my heart. The closeness that I see them share as a family brings about fun and loving memories of my family before all hell broke loose. I can remember Kay asking me what happened to our family. She said she always thought of our family being the "Black Brady Bunch". She remembers us being so happy. My only reply was, things just happen.

But we have to keep faith in God that He is in control.   And as hard as it sounds, know that His word says, ***Romans 8: 28 "And we know that all things work together for good to them that love God, to them who are the called according to his purpose."*** We just have to cherish the good times and know that the bad times were experiences which we can learn from and we must try not to duplicate them. Thank God for Jesus, family, and true friends.

A Lady and Her Two Sons

Our eldest son Rubin is different from his brother and sister in many ways; the family clown. He was the most level headed out of the three children. He came through his teenage years without giving his dad and I much trouble. I believe that was due to us surprising him in seventh grade one day to eat lunch with him and embarrassing him before his friends. (You know that is just not cool with kids) It was then he knew he could always expect us to show up unannounced.

It was not until he graduated from high school when he began to sew his wild oats. Experimenting with what the world had to offer; sex, drugs and alcohol. He gave up on his goals and dreams, dropping out of college and not holding on to a job. After his dad's death, he relied heavily on alcohol, his way of trying to cope.

From jail time, reckless driving, and selling drugs, I never thought that his life would be in this state. It is anguish to my heart to see him this way. However, I trust and believe in faith in God that he will come out of this and become the man the Lord is calling him to be.

Brian's nature was more defiant; curious about how far he could go without getting caught. When he was a little boy he liked to take things apart and put them back together. He was my little handyman. If I needed something put together, Brian was the one.

As a teenager, he and his sister were a lot alike; becoming a parent at a young age of nineteen. Being a father has in some ways slowed Brian down.

The responsibilities which he now faces are beyond just looking out for himself. He now has a daughter to take care of. He now knows all too well how expensive children are. One day he called me to tell me he now can see what his dad and I had to sacrifice for him and his siblings. He thought we never had worries about money. We did not let them see all the hardship, but we did teach them the value of money when they were young. Now that they are older and have responsibilities of their own, they can see what we were trying to instill in them. He told me "momma, I hate to even go to the mail box, bills, bills, bills". I could only laugh and say, "I know!"

I can still picture them as my little boys playing with their sister's hair bows like they were soldier men or playing teenage mutant ninja turtles. Brian breaking his arm jumping out of the tub trying to be Michelangelo or Raphael; one of them turtles. It seems like such a long time ago.

March 13, 2004, a day I will never forget. I had to put the boys out of the house when I needed them the most. The spirit of the Lord showed me that Rubin was selling drugs from our home. Leading up to finding out, there was an unsettling in my spirit that something was going on in the home, but I could not pin point it. I prayed to the Lord to reveal it to me and oh boy did He ever! It was on a Saturday afternoon, I will never forget it. I was on my way to the store when my cell phone rang, it was Debbie. She wanted to come by the house and see the flowers I was making for the banquet. I did not tell her I was on my way to the store; I just turned around and went back to the house.

Prior to finding out about the drugs, I was looking for empty shoe boxes in the house to use for decorations for the banquet. As I picked up a box from Brian's top shelf, I put it back because it felt like it had something in it. While Debbie was still there, the boys came home from work. When she left, I went to the boys' room to talk, shoot the breeze with them before I was leaving to go back to the store again.

I noticed the box that I had seen the day before was now on the dresser. Me thinking it was empty so I could now use it. I looked in it and closed it back because it still had stuff in it. So I walked out of the room getting ready to go to the store, then the Holy Spirit spoke to me, go back and look in the box again. So I did, and to my unbelief and shock, it had packets of marijuana in the box. It took all of the Holy Spirit in me not to swear, I could not believe that my sons would betray me the way they did.   I say sons, because Brian knew about Rubin selling the drugs and did not bother to tell me about it, so at that point; I had to put both of them out of my home.   They were jeopardizing my life and the life of their niece.

I could only imagine my home being broken into by some drugged out junkie or being raided and me going to jail and Kaylianna going to foster care until her mother could come home from Korea. After my rage, I calmed down after talking and praying with my prayer partners; my sisters Annette and Cynthia. I could see the divine intervention of the Holy Spirit and I began to be thankful for listening to that still small whisper.

It has been a month since I had to put the boys out. They came by to pick up some things for their apartment they will be sharing. It was a proud and a sad moment; bittersweet. They are becoming men in the world; taking on their responsibilities which make a mother proud. I know that they felt as though I was being hard on them, but I just did not want them to become momma's boys. I just wanted them to know that I am here for them and will help them in any way I could.

Later that night Kay called, she sounded happy. She was doing well in the army. Her sergeant calls her Mya as did her daddy. She says it is so ironic, him calling her Mya and looking so much like her brother Rubin. Maybe it was what she needed to have in her life to help her to cope with being away from home and losing her father almost a year now.

Riding Out The Storm

The boys are gone, Kay's in the army, I am here
with Kaylianna and there are some days where
I feel so lost and so alone. There are times
when I think, "What did I do to deserve all that
I am going through?" I still ca not believe that
Rubin is gone and the way he left me and the
children, <u>broke, busted and disgusted</u>.

I know that it is only the grace of the Good Lord
that I am still keeping it together in a sense. I
know it is only the human part of me. My flesh
warring against my spirit. I know I have to
realize that things happen and since I love the
Lord and that I am one of the called, I know
that all things are working together for my
good and for His purpose.

If I can just hold on and stay focused, I know I
will make it. I am in a place in my life where I
feel that I am just drifting on a log down the
river not knowing whether to stay on it and
hope for the best, not knowing if I can stand up
against the current of the water or the winds.
The river is getting choppy and I do not know if
I should jump off now and try to swim to dry

land. I never believed that I would be facing what I am facing and not knowing which way the Lord would have me to go. I feel so out of place, like a fish out of water as some might say. They say when you do not know what to do or to say, the best thing to do is to just be still. For how long we ask? Until the Lord says so. How long is that? How will we know it is the Lord telling us to go or to stay? Will we just know? I believe that we will.

He is not the author of confusion, which his word states. He says to acknowledge him in all our ways. Sometimes that is so hard to do because of the warring with our flesh. Lord help! I just want to understand the reasoning behind all of this. I need your guidance Lord. I don't want to fail you. In trying to move on in my life, I could not seem to get it together. I had lost my job, and was going from one temporary job to another. I felt so alone, and decided to sell the house since it became such a struggle and not having help to make ends meet. Kay was in Korea, and it was just Kaylianna and I in the big house.

Prior to selling the house, I went to a Woman Thou Art Loose conference in Atlanta, Georgia with my sister Annette, her friends, Cynthia and sister Brown. While there, I was praying for a miracle. I received a phone call from my realtor that she had sold the house and I needed to be out by the end of the month. That only gave me two weeks to get things sold, packed and placed in storage.

After that was all said and done, my sister Annette and her husband James offered me to come stay with them until I got my head on straight. I took them up on their offer. I loaded up the truck and me and Kaylianna headed to Ft. Myers, Florida. During our brief stay, I got a job working at the post office until I got sick.

When I was feeling somewhat better, I decided to take a little vacation. I dropped Kaylianna off to her grandmother Linda in Groveland, Fl and later took a flight out to Dayton, Ohio to visit my longtime childhood best friend Doris.

After my arrival to Dayton, I started to feel sick again in my body, but I did not let on to her how I was feeling. I did not want to spoil my time with her. It seems like the death of Rubin was getting to me. I was still grieving in a sense and I believe that my body was feeling the stress of it.

The first night that I was there, September 7, 2004, I had another dream about Rubin. I was having them before I left home and they were still continuing. What are they all about? What are these dreams trying to tell me? I just want closure. We went from scene to scene. One minute he is loving on me passionately and the next he is leaving again. He tells me how much he loves and misses me, but then he is gone. It is like I continue to hurt all over again. One scene we were having a disagreement on how my opinion never mattered to him, but if it was his mother's opinion it made sense. It is as though I am still in competition with her even in my dreams. I am just trying to make sense of what the Lord is trying to say to me. It has been almost a year and a half since Rubin's death and I am missing him like crazy. When he was alive we were not close at the end, but I reminisce about the good times we shared. How he made me feel when we made love and how I felt safe in his strong arms as he held me before I rolled over and went off to sleep. That was the one area where we did not have problems. Lord help me to understand what I am going through. It seems as though there is no one I can talk to about what I have gone through and what I am still going through because they have never been through what I have. How can I understand? Is this just my grieving process?

September 8, 2004, dreams, dreams, dreams, another dream about Rubin. Last night he took me for a walk and gave me a wedding band asking me to marry him again because he loves me. Lord, I am trying to make sense of all of this. When we got married the first time at the court house, he did not even buy our wedding rings, I did. I just do not know what to think about all of this. He is gone now and cannot come back; only in my dreams. Why the torture? All the memories, why are they resurfacing? Why are these dreams lingering in my subconscious? On top of all of this, my body is acting crazy. I know I have taken on a lot of stress, but I do not like the way I am feeling. I feel as though I am under an attack from satan, bringing about indigestion and acid reflux. I have prayed to the Lord for my healing and yet I wait. I have also made my peace with the Lord if it is my time to come home and be with him.

There are still so many things I want to do in my life. I want to become a daughter the Lord can be proud of mostly. I would like to travel, ride in a limousine, go to a day spa at a resort and be pampered for a day, and go to an Oprah show. I would also like a new love one day to share my love and life with. I would like for him to be a godly man, fearful of the Lord. I would like for him to be tall and successful enough to take care of me so I will be able to stay home and make his home a safe and loving environment to come home to. I may be asking for too much Lord, but this is what I desire in the man you will send my way.

I know I need my body, mind and spirit healed so I may be the best I can be for the Lord, myself and a new companion. Lord I pray that you would have mercy on me and heal me in all areas of my life that have been so depleted from the attack of satan. Allow me Lord to be strong again for the glory and honor of your name. I want to be whole again! I do not like feeling the way that I am. I need a healing Lord that only you can do. I have thrown up twice today and I still feel as though I need to throw up again.

Picking Up The Debris

James 1: 5 "If any of you lack wisdom, let him ask of God, that giveth to all men liberally, and upbraideth not; and it shall be given him."

If any man lacks wisdom let him ask... In the latter part of our relationship Rubin and I lacked this attribute because we allowed certain forces to come in and deposit negative energy in our lives. Prior to this, we had a loving relationship in many ways. I can truly say that my husband and I loved each other. We had a special relationship, and we were as different as night and day. I was the touchy feeling one, the one always saying that "I love you". He was laid back, but we loved each other in our own way.

It took me a while to come back to these thoughts, remembering how much we did love each other because of the pain, hurt, anger and bitterness that came over me because of the way he left things. Now as I lay here in bed I can only wonder where this journey is taking me. Today is April 18, 2005; the time is rapidly approaching the two year mark of Rubin's death. And as I look back on the past two years, I can truly say "Thank You Lord" for bringing me to the place where I am today. There were times when I felt like giving up, but the Lord would not allow it. I almost gave away my joy; I thank God for Pastors Riva and Zachery Tims who have been feeding my spirit with the word of God. I was having a "valley experience". You ask yourself the question, how do you begin to climb out of the valley? One day at a time.

One must look at past events in one's life to see what situations lead to the valley and then know what to do to come up out of the valley. You have to make up in your mind that you will not allow the devil to run havoc in your life anymore.

Take back your power. Use the power, the
Holy Spirit which God has equipped you with
on the inside to turn your pain and suffering
into helping you get out of the valley so you
will reach your destiny. You have to expose the
devil in the open to regain your true self.
Know that the enemy attacks those who are
going somewhere in the Lord. We are being
attacked because he does not want us to reach
our destiny. He sees our potential, he has
sniffed us out and he smells the anointing on
our lives.

Some people look at the valley as a trying experience of one's soul, body and spirit, which is true. I have tried to look at it as an experience of a life time.

I could not always say that, but when I reached down on the inside, I knew without a shadow of doubt, and with all assurance that Jesus was with me through every situation that I have had to go through. One day I just happen (not by chance) to turn to TBN on a Saturday afternoon and landed on the program Higher Ground. Pastor Riva was speaking about the joy of the Lord is your strength; that I could not have it taken away but, I would have to give it away. It was a "light bulb" moment. The spirit of the Lord leaped inside of me and I knew then that it was my que to get up out of my misery and become alive again. It was time for me to rebound from my pain.

Not only just hearing those words from Pastor Riva encourage me, but I am also reminded of the scripture to encourage myself.

1 Samuel 30: 6 "And David was greatly distressed; for the people spake of stoning him, because the soul of all the people was grieved, every man for his sons and for his daughters: but David encouraged himself in the Lord his God." I know that if it had not been for the Lord, I don't know where I would be today. I was at ground zero, but now I know the Lord is positioning me for a great comeback. "A setback is a set up for a great comeback!"

Moving On

April 24, 2005, it has been two years today that I lost the love of my life. As I am driving to Lakeland this morning to visit the cemetery where Rubin is buried, I felt in my spirit when I awoke to go and make peace and somehow get approval to move on with my life. Although I know it was not necessary in the Spirit, but I felt that it was in the natural. I believe in my heart that it is time to move on, to release myself, my heart from the man who I have loved for over twenty three years as of yesterday; which would have been our twenty-third wedding anniversary.

As I drive through the gates of the cemetery, it being my second encounter of visiting his gravesite; I remember how the first encounter was not so pleasant. As I reflect back I can still recall the phone ringing one morning, it was my friend Carol calling from the funeral home wanting to know if I knew that they were burying Rubin today (since we did not bury him the day of the funeral). No one bothered to inform me, his wife, what was going on. You see, I believed that Rubin's family blamed me for his death. The reason I believed that is because the morning of the funeral, the funeral director called me at my hotel saying that Rubin's family wanted to have an autopsy done. I was so out done. I could only imagine that they thought that foul play was a part of his death, as if I killed him. I was so devastated that they would even think that I would do something like that. But by now they were thinking the worst of me because of the rumors and how our marriage was on the rocks. This was a hurtful time for me with his family. After the funeral we had separate places we ate which was not of my choosing, but theirs. Rubin's family went back to his mother's house. It was an awful feeling. And I know if Rubin could come back, he would say that everything was a mistake and that this is not how things were supposed to be.

The day Rubin died was one of the most devastating days of my life. We had no closure to make things right because we were sleeping in separate bedrooms the night he died. We both were stubborn to the end.

My advice to husbands and wives, take the scripture at heart to never let the sun go down on your wrath. Make things right before you go to bed. I say this because guilt is no one's friend. I felt as though my heart was ripped out of my chest cavity. I can still recall when the paramedic met me coming up the hall to tell me that my husband had passed. I screamed to the point where I heard something pop in my body. What do you do when the one person you love so much is gone? How do you go on? I feel as though I have had an emotional stroke.

Part of me is paralyzed because part of me is gone and now it seems like I am in a malfunctioning mode, just stuck. I took my vows seriously, until death us do part. I was fully committed inspite of the betrayal. I am afraid that I will never get it together again and I know those words go against everything the word of the Lord says, but it is the human part of me.

Where Do I Go From Here??????

I have decided that how far I go in the Lord depends upon my attitude and I know I do not want to be crippled by it. To be crippled is to be partly disabled or lame, to be damaged or defective. And in order for me not to be crippled by my attitude, I know I must continue to walk in the spirit of Jesus Christ. What would cripple my attitude? My way of thinking, leaning to my own understanding instead of letting the mind of Christ rule my being.

Philippians 2: 5, I ask myself the question, what is the mind of Christ Jesus? *Philippians 2: 8 "And being found in fashion as a man, he humbled himself, and became obedient unto death, even the death of the cross."*

I know that I want to be humble before the Lord, mostly in the fear of the Lord, not being afraid kind of fear, but a reverence kind of fear.

I do not want to have the attitude that when things don't go my way, to say I do not have to take this! I have found that there is a reward in humility. *1 Corinthians 2: 9 "Eye hath not seen nor have ear heard nor entered into the heart of man the things which God has prepared for them who love him."*

What would cause damage to my mind? I would say the cares and worries of this life. I must admit that I let some cares and worries get my mind off track when I was left in dire straits. But I thank God for choosing me to be a witness; that I did not remain in that state of mind.

I have always wanted to be an example to be used by the Lord. Strengthen me to do what you would have me to do. Have your way in my life. It is my desire to let my conscious be my guide, yielding to the Spirit of God; for it is the Spirit that will guide us into all truth.

John 16: 13. I live to be truthful to the word and to myself. I do not try to pretend to be something I know I am not. I did not want to be one way in church and at home a different person. I would only be fooling myself. I desire that my attitude be of a sweet disposition. At times we may ask ourselves what is wrong with people. Why do they do the things they do? I have come to the realization that the things I have had to go through were a reality check for me. Those things happened so I could examine myself; so I could fall in line with the word of God in not being so naïve when it comes to people. To be wise enough to know that the wheat and the tare do grow together and it is the Lord that will do the separating.

The ordeal I went through has allowed me to receive a tune-up in Christ; an overhaul you can say. I often wondered what I could have done to have prevented the turmoil that entered into my life.

I mean, I was walking with the Lord, being faithful, and doing all I knew to do to the best of my ability. I know I am not perfect, but I am striving to become the best God would have me to be.

I allowed the enemy to come into the camp when I had the power to resist him. I let my guard down and it was the opportunity for the enemy to come in and to destroy. This was the way I saw it for awhile, but I had to realize that the relationship that I had with my husband was like battling the enemy alone since we had allowed him to come in and destroy our marriage.

We did not go together before the Lord to have him help us in the areas we needed to overcome. He went to his mother and left me to fight alone. I got tired and I will admit in the end I felt like I had lost that battle.

I have now learned the true meaning of the scripture, "leave and cleave in ***Genesis 2: 24.*** ***"Therefore shall a man leave his father and his mother, and shall cleave unto his wife: and they shall be one flesh."***

I can truly look around and say that I am blessed. Even though at times satan tries to persuade me otherwise. I could see how he tries to come against me with envy and jealousy. I am thankful to the Lord for putting things in perspective for me. I could see myself getting angry with my husband dying and leaving me in such a desperate situation. On one particular day I was with two of my friends and they were able to shop till their hearts were content, having husbands who adore them and they could basically do what they wanted with money and here I was not even able to buy a pack of gum. I know my husband did not have control over him dying, but he did have the control on how he left things. Leaving the kids and I without any financial support. Even after I filed the bankruptcy, it still did not help me to get back on my feet. There were things they did not take off of my credit report and now I still cannot get credit anywhere. I try not to think about it, but some days I do get frustrated and angry. Not because I want to shop till I drop, but because I felt I have done all the right things in life after the Lord saved me. I treated people the way I wanted to be treated even if I was treated badly, helping where there was a need and not looking for a pat on the back, just to be secure in the Lord. I had to check myself and not get discouraged. I must say there are some days when I don't feel like the Lord has my back. I know those emotions stems from the enemy. I know I cannot go on my emotions or my feelings. I must continue to hold on to my faith no matter how much it is tested. Through these storms in my life, I cannot stop in the middle, but I must outlast the storms.

There have been many struggles since Rubin's death, mostly financial. Two and a half years and I still cannot get a decent break. If I take one step forward, the devil seems to knock me two to three steps back. Going from paycheck to paycheck, juggling one bill to the next, however, in the midst of the turmoil, I am ever so determined to stay faithful in the Lord. No matter what I see around me with my natural eyes, but I must look towards heaven with my spiritual eyes knowing that the best is yet to come! I must stay focused in order to see clearly, looking further than I can see. For the just live by faith and not by sight. I have to see myself past the difficult times. I cannot look at what is in front of me. It is like you have to have a binocular kind of vision in this walk with the Lord. Looking beyond what you can see in the natural. The one thing I want to hang on to is my ability to stay humble before the Lord.

God's strength was made perfect in my weakness. When I felt hopeless, depressed, suicidal, abandoned, I had to continue to abide in the word of God with a glimmer of hope. I had to believe that God is about to do something in my life. I do not have to beg God to do anything for me.

Sometimes I would find myself asking the question, how long will it be before the Lord does what he promises to do especially when you do not see any relief in sight. When it seemed as though things were not getting any better, that is when I had to rely even more on my faith.

In his word, John 15: ...if we abide in him and let his word abide in us, that we can ask what we will and it will be given to us. And in asking for what we will, we must also believe in faith that it will come to pass.
It is all about Jesus. Even in my darkest of times, I am so grateful that I know him. After everything I have been through, I can still say "Thank You Lord!"

When the problems which seemed so overwhelming came, I knew that I could not give up, throw in the towel or even run away to a place where there was no stress, somewhere that no one knew me or my name. I knew that I could not panic, but I had to hold on to the promises of God. I could not renege on my commitment I have made unto him. I had to remain focused and loyal, I had to hang tough even when the trouble in my life seemed so detrimental.

My commitment to the Lord is to be reliable, faithful and trustworthy. My desire is to be wholly devoted to the Lord through thick and thin. It has been over two and a half years now that I have been celibate. I am grateful to the Lord for keeping me, which is my desire to be kept. Fornication or masturbation is not an option for me. I do not want to forfeit my blessings from the Lord where I would allow my flesh to dictate to me what my body wants. The time will come again when I will say "I Do", but until then I shall remain celibate. Sure I get lonely at times for companionship and intimacy; after being with one man for twenty-one years it gets hard at times, but I thank God for being the lover of my soul. I know him to be a keeper of the mind, body, soul and spirit. I have made up in my mind to hold on until my change has come, and while holding on I will continue to walk in the spirit. *Galatians 5: 16 "This I say then, walk in the Spirit, and ye shall not fulfill the lust of the flesh."*

Jesus More Than Life To Me
By: Dorothy Davis Collins

Jesus, you're more than life to me,
You're the one who set me free.
Whom the Son set free us free indeed,
For only you can supply my every need.

Day in and day out, sometimes not
Knowing just what to do,
Realizing I have a cross to bear
If I intend to follow you.

The pathways I've taken
Not as bright as I've desired them to be
But half the battle is won
Because the Son has set me free.

The joy and center of my life,
Jesus you are,
Trusting and believing in you by faith
I know I will travel far.

Just Before The Breaking Point

Be of good courage and He will strengthen thy heart...impartation from the Lord

Just when you are on the verge of giving up, hold on for your blessings which are at hand. There are times when you feel like you cannot go on and you cannot see or feel the reason to go on, just remember you cannot go by your feelings, an emotion which can be very deceiving. You fear you have no more rope to hold on to. Tie a knot at the end of that rope and keep on hanging on.

For the Lord did not give us the spirit of fear, but of love, power and of a sound mind. Giving up is not an option. I thank God for His love which is surrounding me. If we keep the mind of Christ we will triumph victoriously. ***Phil 2: 5 "Let this mind be in you which was also in Christ Jesus...*** Our attitude should be as Christ.

When you wake in the morning and your children seem as though they do not belong to you, that you did not birth or raise them, hang on! When chaos on the job reaps havoc on you, hold on! When your husband or your wife do not treat you the way they should, hold on! When you are deep in debt, hold on! Help is on the way. These things did not just happen overnight, they are daily mind games deposited by our enemy and if we do not address them on a daily basis with prayer, fasting, praise, faithfulness, they will invade our lives and we become unproductive for the Lord. There will be times that seem unbearable, but do not give up; because just before the breaking point, when you think you cannot go any further, Jesus is there, for He is an on time God.

There are lessons to be learned just before the breaking point, lessons that we feel are too great to bear, again I say, we cannot go by our feelings. The Lord knows what we are able to bear even before satan accuses us before him, therefore, we are to prove him wrong and to God be the glory.

A lot of times when we have been accused by satan, all we have to do is resist him and he will flee. However, we must have maintained a good fitting of our armour before his attack, arming ourselves with the word of God, which is our weapon to sustain. We can never think we can defeat our enemy without the most important weapon, God's word.

This Too Will Pass
By: Dorothy Davis Collins

Fiery darts from one's kindled tongue
With fierce words of hurt and pain,
Leaves you wondering
Why me Dear Lord, why all the blame?

Hurt, pain, many sorrows and grief to bear,
Learning day by day to take them to the altar
Endeavoring to leave them there.

The temporary release of tears I've shed,
Knowing you will wipe them all away
I'm holding on, not giving up,
For tomorrow will be a brighter day.

For your name sake Lord, the trials and tribulations
And false accusations I will take,
Just as the wind, not knowing which way they
Come and go
A better and stronger inner me will they make.

Striving for excellence, wanting desperately to
Please you in every way,
Reaching for the promise shore, where the
Blessings of Joy and Peace are present each day.

A Special Tribute

I pay tribute in this book to my father in the gospel, the late Apostle Henry Ross, Sr.; a lover of souls. Words cannot express the love I had for my pastor, who taught me the word of God. Who taught me and others by example on how to pray, live holy and how to die.

I can recall when Apostle Ross had become stricken with cancer and was taken to his bed; he was a man who loved the Lord so much that he had them bring him to church on a stretcher so he could come and fellowship with the people one more time before his death.

He was a man of great integrity and character who loved the Lord, his family, congregation and his community. He truly had a love of souls.

Being under his ministry was like sitting at the feet of Jesus, listening to every word of God which came forth to bless my soul and spirit.

I can recall one night of service where at the end he called everyone up to the altar to pray for us. I vividly remember as he was laying on of hands, I could see the glory of the Lord on him. It was a blessing to see God having favor upon his mighty servant.

The love I have for him will always be in my heart.

Special Thanks

When going through the rough patches in my life, I did not have the desire to attend church on a regular basis. I became a bedside member in the army of the Lord. This was a time I needed to retreat; to come back refreshed and renewed.

I received the word of God from many pastors and evangelists. Bishop T. D. Jakes, a special message entitled "Silent Frustrations" really spoke to my spirit along with Pastor Paula White's message "Can You Stand To Be Blessed", and others such as Dr. Creflo & Taffi Dollar, Dr. Juanita Bynum, Pastor Joel Osteen, James & Betty Robison, Joyce Meyer and Dr. Zachary and Riva Tims of New Destiny Christian Center where I attended when Rubin passed away were also encouraging words from the Lord for my soul and spirit. I thank God for the Trinity Broadcast Station with Paul and Jan Crouch and the Word Network.

Dr. B. J. Releford founder of Women of Power, an organization of women from all walks of life and denominations helping women to empower themselves and walk in power in the Lord.

My psalmist of praise from Donnie McClurkin, I would listen to him as my heart, soul and spirit was lifted up to help ease the hurt and pain. My favorite song of praise, "Stand".

These men and women of God helped me in so many ways to keep looking up to God, knowing that He will bring me out in due season.

Special thanks to Sarah Grace of Ingenuity Enterprises for helping me implement the vision I had for the book cover and for the photo of my mother and father. She is a God-send.

Special recognition to my co-worker, Jane Genge-Nizic, who helped me in transferring the documents from the floppy disc to the flash drive due to my lack of computer technology.

Also, a special thanks to my granddaughter Kaylianna for her contribution of the author's photo on the back cover.

To my special daughter, Kayamia "Mya" Collins, thank you so much for editing the book. I know it was challenging. I just want you to know how much I love you and appreciate your help.

Love Letter To My Husband

April 23, 2013

My dearest Rubin,

Oh how I loved you. It has taken me ten years to complete this book. I have had many distractions along the way. Often wondering how this part of my journey unfolded the way it did. I have thought about you often down through the years, every April 23, 24 and 25th, hoping that one day it would all make sense to me.   All I can come up with is, it is what it is and was suppose to be. Nevertheless, I only hoped that you knew how much I loved you. We would have celebrated our 31st wedding anniversary today. I had always pictured us growing old together with the love of our children and grandchildren by our side.

It has been a struggle for all of us since your death, feeling abandoned and unloved. There was a hole in all of our hearts which have taken years of healing. Perhaps you did love us in your own way, but we struggled nevertheless. I hope you knew how much I tried to please you in every way. How I tried to cater to you as my king. I took the vows in our marriage to heart and I tried to be the best wife, lover and friend to you; and a good mother to our children. I know we had some rough times in the marriage, but I loved you still. With much love I deeply regret not being there at the end for you due to our stubbornness. That was a very hard lesson I had to learn from, oh the guilt!

I hope and believe that this book will be a help to many women and men in relationships; whether they are married or just dating. Realizing the importance of having open communication in the relationship; to be open and honest with one another.

To have a love with one another that makes each other feel safe, so when the enemy comes to try and break down the relationship you know that you have one another's back. To know that you can stand the test of time "until death us do part". I pray that what I have gone through is not in vain, but God has received the glory out of it all. I will always love you Rubin.

Love,

Dorothy